TRUMP
IS MY QUARTERBACK
AKA PRESIDENT

TRUMP
IS MY QUARTERBACK
AKA PRESIDENT

THE G.O.A.T OF U.S. PRESIDENTS

BRIAN E. DAVIS

PALMETTO
PUBLISHING
Charleston, SC
www.PalmettoPublishing.com

Hardcover ISBN: 9798822960619
Paperback ISBN: 9798822960626

Contents

FOREWORD FROM THE AUTHOR

First and foremost, Thank You for purchasing my book. Just a few tidbits about myself: I'm a life-long Chicagoan and an avid sports fan, especially the American version of Football, I'm talking about Sunday and Monday night football!

I went to *The University of Chicago. I walked the halls where Milton Friedman taught. I also went to *Northwestern University's Medill School of Journalism. I left both Universities with the prestigious Distinction of EE, Expeditor Extraordinaire. In other words, I am a truck driver.

I think being President is somewhat akin to being a quarterback. I have been waiting a very long time for my favorite team, the Chicago Bears to find a quarterback. As of today, I am anointing Donald Trump as My Quarterback!

*I was never a student at the aforementioned universities. I was there in another capacity.

It's the 2024 Presidential Election and the stakes are extremely high. Through the use of lampooning, facts, satirizing and parodying Joe Biden, Kamala Harris and the Democrats, the authors mission is to help promote and campaign for Donald Trump to win back the Whitehouse.

INTRODUCTION

"Trump was right about NATO. Trump was kinda right about immigration. He grew the economy quite well. His tax reform worked. He was right about some of China. He wasn't wrong about some of these critical issues."

Jaime Dimon,
Chairman and CEO of JP Morgan Chase

THE QUARTERBACK SIGNALS

"Two- 42, Twenty-16, Twenty-24, Set, Hut, Hut!"

For the women that would like to join in, here is your play signals:

"Shake and bake, Peach Cobbler, Peach Cobbler, Oklahoma, ready, set, Go !"

CHAPTER 1

PUT #46, BIDEN ON THE BENCH

Due to foreseen circumstances, our current quarterback is failing and falling every time you look around. He has no energy and he has too many bogus business transactions.

He is fucking terrible, put his ass on the bench. On second thought, put his ass on waivers.

We need the All-World Pro, Donald John Trump at the helm. Back in the day, there was the legendary Johnny Unitas and Joe Namath. At 77 years old, Donald Trump still has the arm strength and he can run to McDonalds for a cheese-burger in twenty two seconds flat. He still has the mindset to out think his opponents and critics. Most of all, it's his leadership skill set that makes him the only choice to have both footballs in his hands.

Without a doubt, after his quarterback days are done, he has all the attributes to become a force in the business world. Perhaps even a football team owner. All of the sports writers share this opinion about my quarterback; he is a winner and champion. Even the political and sports critics can't get enough of his swag, they love him. It's kinda like a Muhammad Ali and Howard Cosell thing, they need each other. You might want to include Jim Acosta and Donald Trump, they love one another too.

Change at the quarterback position is coming. We need a QB to get us to the United States best policies zone and score touchdowns. "Don Unite Us, Don Unite Us!"

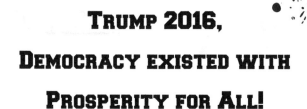

TRUMP 2016,
DEMOCRACY EXISTED WITH
PROSPERITY FOR ALL!

TRUMP 2024,
DEMOCRACY STILL **EXIST**, AND THERE
WILL BE PROSPERITY FOR ALL AGAIN!

VOTE TRUMP 2024

CHAPTER 2

GREATEST PLAYFAKE EVER

The Greatest Play Fake Ever. Get Ready folks, here comes another highlight story about The Goat, Tom Brady, right? Nope. My fellow voters I want you to etch this play in your mind and remember it all the way until it's time to vote for the 2024 Presidency. Here is the name of the play:

It's called, Kingmaker to Not Ready for Prime Time presidential candidate. The two featured players are named Joe Biden and James Clyburn.

Just to refresh your minds, this is when James Clyburn endorsed Joe Biden and saved his candidacy, which was on life support. In essence, this event is the genesis of all the Bullshit we are dealing with now, which includes inflation, crime, open borders, war, layoffs and more.

During my research, I came across a quote from Mr. James Clyburn that resonated with me. The following is the statement:

"Our challenge is making the greatness of this country accessible and affordable for all."

This statement resonated with me because this is exactly what My Quarterback accomplished during his first term. I'm talking about Donald Trump!

My fellow voters, disregard the personality of My Quarterback and focus on the record and the performance. Let me also add, Donald Trump is the only President whose policies were a win-win for the whole world. Joe Biden did not bring back normalcy, he single handily fucked it up.

Here is another quote from Mr. James Clyburn that resonated with me:

"I'm fearful for my daughters and their future and their children and their children's future."

The Washington Post By Donna M. Owens
April 1, 2020

While the two statements from Mr. Clyburn were from the 2020 Presidential Primary race season, the statement regarding the future of his daughters resonates to me as it relates to the current February 2024 news cycle. Let me be 100% clear, President Biden has blood on his hands because of his open border policies. Illegal immigrants are crossing our borders unvetted and are committing heinous crimes against infant girls, young women, police officers and the general public. Mr. President you own this problem, period.

CHAPTER 3

PRESIDENT #44 AND PRESIDENT #45, THE PROGNOSTICATORS

Perhaps President Trump and President Obama foresaw something in the future that many voters, especially Democratic voters did not. President Obama once famously stated, "Don't underestimate Joe's ability to fuck things up." Of course, My Quarterback knew this well ahead of everyone, even before he became President. The following is a listing of just a few of Joe Bidens colossal fuck ups:

1. President Biden administration frivolous spending has caused hyperinflation.

2. He made us more dependent on Russian uranium. Joe Biden restricted development on more than 1 million acres of land that includes the only U.S. source of high-grade uranium ore. Since the United States is the largest purchaser of Russian enriched uranium, the move increases our dependence on Russia at a time when we are trying to isolate from Vladimir Putin.

3. He circumvented the Supreme Court on student loan forgiveness with the stroke of a pen, Biden tried in 2022 to cancel half a trillion dollars in student debt, only to see his unconstitutional plan blocked by the Supreme Court. So Biden used other regulatory means to write off nearly $132 billion in student debt anyway effectively forcing blue collar workers to subsidize the higher education of white collar professionals and launching a frontal assault on Congress power of the purse.

4. He failed to police antisemitism on the left. When Biden declared his candidacy for President in 2019, he condemned the right-wing bigots in Charlottesville, chanting the same antisemitic bile heard across Europe in the 30's. Yet he failed to forcefully confront the explosion of antisemitic bile on the left from college campuses to Capitol Hill, after Hamas October 7 terrorist attack on Israel.

5. He allowed a Chinese spy balloon to violate U.S. Airspace. For days, the Biden administration did nothing to stop the 20 story Chinese craft until someone in Montana looked up at the sky and said : "What the hell is that?" Even Democrats including former defense secretary and CIA director Leon Pannetta called out Joe Biden for letting it sail over our country for a week before finally shooting it down over the Atlantic.

6. He allowed the worst border crisis in U.S. history to get even worse. In fiscal 2023, the record for the most encounters at the southern boarder was broken for the third straight year. Just before Christmas, there were more than 12,600 migrant encounters in a single day, the highest total ever recorded. A December Wall Street Journal poll found that 64 percent disapprove of Bidens boarder policies, while just 27 percent approve.

7. He blocked allies from giving Ukraine a clear path to NATO membership. At a July summit in Vilnius , Lithuania, a majority of NATO allies wanted to set a specific timetable for Kyivs admission into the alliance, but Biden rejected their entreaties in fear of provoking Russia-giving Putin a major victory. It's the same flawed reasoning that has led Biden to withhold critical weapons Ukraine needs to retake it's territory.

8. The withdrawl from Afghanistan, the Super-Colossal Tragedy Failure.

*The Washington Post
By Marc A. Thiessen
The 10 worst things President Biden did in 2023
December 29, 2023

Tired of Democrats taking Your

Vote for Granted

Vote Trump

2024

CHAPTER 4

THE PLAY: DOUBLE REVERSE TAX DOLLARS

Our borders are constantly being bombarded with illegal migrants. This situation is overwhelming our resources. Illegal migrants are coming from all over the world to try to enter the United States of America. How long can the U.S. withstand this influx of legal and illegal migrants? There was one report that stated we are spending $9,000.00 per illegal alien. This is more than what we are spending on our Veterans. This is totally insane.

Once the illegal migrants are in America, various states are housing, feeding, providing school for their children and more. Let me be 100% clear, I am pro legal immigration. Prior to the influx and invasion of illegals entering our country, resources were already scarce, especially in minority communities. These are our tax dollars being allocated to people who are not citizens and have not paid one red cent in taxes.

To add injury to insult, most of these illegal migrants home country receive our U.S. tax dollars from U.S. financial aid agencies and non-government organizations. So in essence, we are providing financial assistance before the fact and after. These illegal migrants are getting paid over and over again. I would bet that a lot of the money is sent back to their home country to relatives because of the surplus of tax dollars.

One of the most prominent agencies that is proactive with financial aid around the globe is *USAID. If you were given a breakdown of the illegal migrants home country and the vast amount of financial aid or our tax money that are sent all over the world to help citizens in their own country, the dollar amounts are astronomical. For example, on February 15, 2023, the United States announced there would be forthcoming additional aid of $42.5 million collectively for the people of El Salvador, Guatemala and Honduras. Keep our tax dollars at home, put America first. Let's spend our tax dollars in a great judicious manner again and not frivolously.

*U.S. Agency for International Development

CHAPTER 5

DEMOCRATIC PLAYBOOK FOR MY QB

"If We Don't":

- Tackle
- Impeach Trump
- Clip
- Block
- Cheat
- Indict Trump
- Trip
- Blitz
- Rough the Passer
- Interfere
- Create Bogus Russian Stories
- Jump Off-Slides
- Create Lawfare
- Create False Rape Cases

"He is going to be Re-elected"

Tired of High Crime Rate in Your Neighborhood

Vote Trump

2024

CHAPTER 6

TRUMP DERANGEMENT SYNDROME LIVE!

Congratulations to all of the 2024 graduates around the country. I always wonder what celebrities and officials will appear at these commencement events and give the keynote speech. Will it be Oprah, Robert Smith, Jerry Seinfield, a football kicker from K.C., local politician or a national politician.

You would never guess who was a keynote speaker at the graduation I was in attendance at. Since I'm an ex -democrat, I'm going to put on a Trump Derangement Syndrome Hat. Let me flashback to H-town, Houston, Texas in 2018. Well folks, time to get mad and angry.

"If you see a Maga follower out and about you get in their face and give them a piece of your mind. If you see them at a restaurant, you take their beans and brussel sprouts, they don't deserve to fart, subsequently, this will also reduce climate change. If you see them at a bank, you go tell that teller to go find William Tell to hit them in the behind with an arrow." If you don't know now, I am talking about Mrs. Maxell Cassette!

According to the conversations I had with some of the 2018 graduates, they felt her speech was too angry and most of all very uninspiring.

DRILL BABY DRILL!!

TRUMP 2024

CHAPTER 7

TRUMP DERANGEMENT SYNDROME, PART 2

Here we go again. Another keynote speaker that is immensely uninspiring and angry. This Historical and Prestigious School, Morehouse College chooses "Mr. they gonna put y'all back in chains" Joe Biden as the keynote speaker. Five seconds into his keynote speech, President Gaffy (Joe Biden) starts with the identity politics' bullshit. "The black man gotta work one-hundred times harder than the whole world or some other bullshit" like you can't be successful because of the system. Why not lead with a more positive message Mr. President. It's always race crap with the Democrats.

I think a better keynote speech would start with a simple and genuine Congratulations. From that point, to all of the 2024 graduates, opportunity is everywhere. Work hard and strive for excellence. Innovate and add value in your respective careers.

Better yet, why don't you look at Donald Trump's commencement address and follow his lead. Just check out a YouTube video.

You want Cheaper Gas Prices?

Vote Trump

2024

CHAPTER 8

THE SPORTS REPORTER

"Hey Joe, what about that referee call in that football game? Do you think it was illegal procedure on the running back or an undocumented procedure?"

"Hey Joe, why did you fuck up the border when my Quarterback fixed it?"

"Hey Joe, who is your favorite football coach, is it Lincoln Riley?"

"Hey Joe, what was the plan in Afghanistan, come one, come all desperately at once?"

BAD PLAN JOE

"Hey Joe, what's up with the transitory, still running away inflation."

"Hey Joe, the interest rates are too damn high."

"Hey Joe, when was the last time you went grocery shopping?"

"Hey Joe, do you think I can establish 50 shell companies in Delaware to conceal my NON-Fara-compliant business transactions, sounds kinda illegal and undocumented."

"Hey Joe, number 46, you must be one of those smooth criminals."

"How about getting me one of those sole sourced contracts or maybe just a set aside one for me, the no bidding one of course."

"I hear the family business is good and that you're off on Wednesdays. "

"Make it happen Bro, holla back, preferably by November 5, 2024."

"Time is running out for you Grand Bro!"

TIRED OF YOUR GROCERIES COSTING

$500.000 A WEEK

VOTE TRUMP

2024

CHAPTER 9

VIRTUE SIGNALINGVILLE

Every state has a town or two or three and so on that have residents that virtue signals.

They are located on the eastside, westside, northside and the southside of each city and suburb. As I earlier stated, I am a truck driver/courier. I make pick-ups and deliveries throughout my home state of Illinois. I'm sure you have come across or might even reside in a town where some of the resident's virtue signal. These are the cities and towns of "Love." The residents profess to love everybody and everything. You've seen the signs in the windows and lawns that state "Love is Love", "Black Lives Matter", "Every Human is Legal and Hate has No Home Here." The aforementioned statements are proof and positive you are in a neighborhood full of crazy liberal progressive lefties. Hell, even some of the pets and nature's animals in these town's display crazy liberal progressive tendencies and attitudes.

Based upon my personal experience of doing delivery routes throughout the state of Illinois, allow me to give you the low down on these crazy liberal progressive lefty towns. Before I go any further, let me reveal my ethnicity so you can really understand my plight. Can I get a drumroll and jellyroll, I got a sweetooth don't you know. Well folks here we go, the big reveal, I am BLACK! I am a well-groomed man, and I must say a rather handsome lad. My uniform is always clean and of course I always render professional service. Yet, the following occurrences depicts how a routine delivery transaction can morph into semi-racial, absolute racial, hate and quite frankly, some plumb crazy overtures from the people "full of love, respect, and tolerance":

Today's route takes me to a prominent and affluent Western Suburb of Chicago. Let's get racial. The following action happens everywhere there are lefties, and not just this town. I pull up to this beautiful home to deliver their package. The screen door is closed but the security door is wide open. Some of the ground level windows are open to let in fresh air. I make the delivery. Before I could take two steps toward my bright delivery truck, all the windows are closed with the quickness and the security door is slammed closed and locked, is this the "Love" that I am feeling? Hell to the NO, its not. These are the main people who call my My Quarterback, a racist.

Another day and another route. Today's route take me to another prominent and affluent western suburb of Chicago. Ironically, this towns shopping center has been hit with a lot of smash and grab crimes and robberies. The crazy liberal progressive's policies of Chicago is causing issues for this affluent town. Here we go. I make my delivery to this palatial home. The male resident is cordial and signs for the package. I say good morning to the lady in the driveway getting out of her Bentley Continental GT and she ignores my greeting and walks on by. I see the "Black Lives Matter" sign in the lawn. Once again, is this the "LOVE" that I'm feeling? I'm starting to feel like David Coverdale though. Hell to the no, it's not Love.

Back at it again, today's route takes me to a far western suburb of Chicago. This town has a national reputation as being one of the best towns to live in. Let's get to it.

I know from past deliveries that this express letter is hot and urgent. I approach the front door, suddenly I hear a voice coming from one of those fancy doorbells that the owner can see and communicate with visitors to their home. The male voice shouts out the following statement "I'm not interested and get off my property." Mind you, I'm in uniform. I adhere to his request and left the property and went back to my truck to head to the next delivery stop. As I pulled off heading down the street, the owner of the home with the fancy doorbell came running, sorta like Usain Bolt. Without a doubt, this guy was closer to Usain Boat than Usain Bolt. He was too overweight to catch me. Furthermore, I increased my speed and pretended I did not see "Mr. Get Off of My Property." I tried to deliver his passport but he saw my skin color before my uniform colors, LMAO(Laughing My Ass Off)!

TIRED OF ILLEGAL IMMIGRATION

VOTE FOR TRUMP

2024

CHAPTER 10

LOONEY LAW PALOOZA:

Inspired by the bogus cases brought against President Trump by District Attorney and Attorney Generals

"Welcome to the show ladies and gentlemen! Let's get this show started!"

"Introducing!

Jack Sham & The Black Supremist, featuring the AG's (All Goons) and the DA's (Dumb Asses).

On lead vocals we have Jack Sham singing his super flop song, "I wish I had a case."

"Laying that bottom **DOWN AND OUT** on the bass, Annie Willing.

On the Drums we have Dr. Always out of time, but twinkie time.

On Lead Guitar, we have Lola Jones giving it everything she got while trying to take everything you fucking got."

"Coming to your town Check out the Tour dates:

August 4, 2024 (Cancelled due to lack of ticket sales)

September 4, 2024 (Cancelled due to lack of ticket sales)

October 4, 2024 (Cancelled due to lack of ticket sales)

November 5, 2024 (Cancelled because bandmembers were thrown in jail)"

Chapter 11

Flag on the field, Personal Foul on the Democrats

The call on the field is personal foul on the Democrats for illegally trying remove President Trump from the Presidential election Ballot. The next personal foul will result in the Democratic Presidents removal from the Ballot.

Tired of All the Fentanyl Deaths

Vote Trump

2024

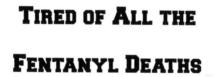

CHAPTER 12

THE GAME DISRUPTER

Like Andrew Luck in his first year in the NFL, My QB changed the game like no other rookie since Andrew Luck. Ever since Trump came down the escalator in 2015, he has been a force to be reckon with. When you are an international business developer of the highest order, you conduct business directly with the heads of state. In essence, this makes you a Geo-political player. His accomplishments on the field and in the political space is unassailable. Perhaps his swag and his get the job done persona is what created the never-Trump-ster hate and jealousy. Furthermore, his ability and vision to anticipate the defense, global events and call the right play makes him stand out from the has beens and never has beens.

Stay tune folks for the next few years. Trump is definitely My Quarterback and he should be Yours!

Chapter 13

Flagg on the Field, Taunting On The Blue Team (Democrats)

The following are some of the ridiculous names the Democrats have called My Quarterback:

- "Hitler"
- "Orange Man"
- "Fascist"
- "Racist"
- "Mussolini"
- "Useful Idiot"
- "Autocrat"
- "Dictator
- "Existential Threat"

And so on....

This is the reason I left the Democratic Party, and it should be yours. We need politicians to discuss the issues and challenges we deal with every day and how they can make our lives better.

The bullshit buffoonery of calling the opposite party names does not address the issues. As voters we need a criteria to make the best assessment of a candidate for them to earn our vote!

You want School Choice

Vote for Trump

2024

CHAPTER 14

BROKEN WINDOWS, BROKEN CITIES

My kinda of town, Chicago is my kinda of town, pause the singing ole Blue eyes, aka Frank Sinatra. Chicago is not your kinda of town anymore. It's fucked up and full of crime throughout the city. As a lifelong Chicagoan, I've always loved this city, it's a world desired destination. As of this writing, she is a broken city. We need Law and Order. One of my favorite things to do in downtown Chicago is hang out on the Mile, the Gold Coast and the corner of Lasalle and Madison. The location of Lasalle and Madison is where my favorite men's haberdashery, *Syd Jerome* is located.

As a truck driver, I cannot afford most of the suits sold there, but dammit I like to window shop. Ever since the George Floyd riots, the store has been looted or burglarized 4 times. Instead of displaying fine menswear, at times the windows are boarded up or completely opaque. There is no need to visit Atlantic City's boardwalk, we have our own fricking boardwalk, except the boards are vertical. On to the Mile, The Magnificent Mile, is Chicago's premier commercial district. The vibrant, bustling area is home to upscale shops, luxe fashion outlets, cool restaurants, and posh hotels. All of these descriptors describing the Mile is 100% accurate. Unfortunately, the city is being ruined by the policies of leftist ideologies ruling the city and state. Do you hear me Mr. Mayor,Mr./Mrs Cook County State Attorney and Mr. Governor?

The following below are just a few of the many crimes that have occurred on the Magnificent Mile:

- 4 suspects used their 5 finger credit cards and made off with some luxury hand bag from Burberry
- A Group of robbers break into Michigan Avenue MAC make-up store
- Five unknown offenders entered Gucci and stole product from within before fleeing in a vehicle

Mr-Mag-com
August 14, 2020

Abc 7 Chicago Digital Team
Wednesday August 16, 2023

Fox 32 Chicago
By Kasey Chronis
April 4, 2022

CHAPTER 15

COMMITTED, BUT NOT REALLY

My QB, Donald John Trump is committed to keeping America safe and prosperous. My QB is also committed to our international allies. Unlike this current administration under Joe Biden and in typical Democratic Fashion, they are not fully committed to our country and its international allies.

As an ex-democratic voter, myself and other minorities have been waiting for decades for the Democrats, to be fully and completely committed to our needs and concerns throughout this country.

You want to build

Generational Wealth

Vote for Trump

2024

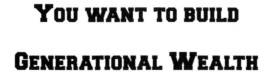

CHAPTER 16

THE TRIANGLE OF COVER-UP:

Welcome to the Triangle of Cover-Up. The Triangle of cover-up includes the legacy media, gas lighters on cable and the entire Democratic Party. According to the unimpressive White House press-say lady, Joe Biden boogie boards all the way across the Atlantic Ocean to the United Kingdom and then swims the English Channel in 60 minutes.

She claims that no one in the office can keep up with speedy Joe Biden. Perhaps Joe Biden can participate in the Paris Olympics. Go for the gold Joe, the gold Jeritol with ginseng. Mrs. Press-say lady, I have a question for you. The bag of cocaine that was found in the Whitehouse, did you snort a couple of lines of cocaine? Surely, you can't expect us to believe the athleticism Joe Biden displays before 7:00 o'clock am. You can't be serious Mrs. Press-Say lady.

On and on to the break of dawn. The gas lighters on cable and the Trump hating channels tells us that Joe Biden is at the top of his game. "He is better than mom's apple pie. We have known him for fifty years and I've never seen him sharper." It is very obvious that the entire Democratic party have been sharing the same bag of cocaine found inside the Whitehouse. Speaking of cover-up, funny how that case went unsolved.

Let it be written that the gas lighters on cable, the legacy media and the entire democratic party are all complicit in this cover-up for the ages. Mr. and Mrs. CEO of the networks should have buyer's remorse. Where have your professional standards gone? When your viewership dwindles down to nothing, you will be lucky to get a Nelson rating, let alone a Nielson rating. Take your overpaid anchorman and women and go back to school.

Promises Made, Promises Achieved

Vote for Trump

2024

Chapter 17

Vice President G.G. Giggles Part 1:

"By the time I walk to Milwaukee, the time will pass by. By the time I walk back from Milwaukee, the time will pass by. When I was walking back from Milwaukee the northern wind was blowing to the north. As I made it south of Milwaukee, the southern wind was blowing to the south. As I headed to the east, the easterly wind was blowing east. When I made a left turn 10 miles from where I was at, I found myself heading west. Who would have thunk it. As I headed west, the westwind was blowing west. All of this passage of time and there will be no presidency of mine. There's always lunch! I will have a word salad."

Inspired by Vice President Passage of Time Speech

Vote For the Party of

Law and Order

Vote Trump

2024

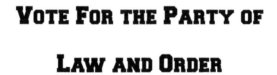

CHAPTER 18

VICE PRESIDENT G.G. GIGGLES PART 2:

"Hello my fellow Americans. I want to win your vote. I'm running for the Presidency now. It appears that some special interest people are scrubbing from the internet the accomplishments Joe and I achieved. Feel free to read the following listing. We do not want the American people to forget our record:

- We doubled the mortgage cost
- We caused families to fall behind on bills
- We caused hyperinflation
- We caused historic high interest rates
- We caused real wages to fall
- We caused families to shrink their savings "

Kamala Harris must answer and be held accountable for the open borders and the financial debilitating inflation she caused.

To the American voter, do not let Kamala Harris off the hook. Vote for Donald Trump. He has proven by actual real performance and a successful record that he is the only choice for President. Furthermore, Kamala Harris is an extreme liberal socialist. I recommend doing a basic YouTube search and hear Kamala Harris state word for word her socialistic views.

Vote for Trump 2024!

CHAPTER 19

10 MINUTES AGO, KAMALA

10 minutes ago Kamala, you and President Biden let millions of illegal migrants into the interior of the United States, without any vetting process.

10 minutes ago Kamala, millions of single mothers went to the grocery store to buy food for their families and could barely afford to buy one can of spam and a bag of apples. Why? Because of the inflationary policies you and Joe Biden implemented.

10 minutes ago Kamala, you were asked some challenging questions by a reporter, per usual, when you don't have a viable answer, it's laughing time.

10 minutes ago Kamala, you said Joe Biden is at the top of his game. Right.

10 minutes ago Kamala, your approval rate was lower than Joe Biden's.

Perhaps during the *Passage of Time,* the current Democratic voter's, will realize its MAGA TIME, VOTE FOR TRUMP 2024!

Tired of the Crime on the Public Transportation System

Vote Trump

2024

Chapter 20

The Screen Play:

At all levels of American Football, the screen play is one of the most effective plays to get a touchdown. Just imagine Barry Sanders catching the football in the backfield, then juking his way down the field for the touchdown. Wow!

On June 27, 2024 in Atlanta, Georgia, Joe Biden called for a right screen. From that point on, the night was a total disaster. The screen play was doomed from the start. From the way he shuffled his feet to get up to the podium, to his wife assisting him to walk off the stage, all of three steps. In between the beginning and ending of the debate, there was just as many troubling and startling actions by the current President, Joe Biden. For example, his words were spoken in an incoherent way. The train of thought was not there which is not good especially when the world was watching. The President must exemplify strength and stability.

Father time eventually catches up to all of us. Most observers have noticed the health decline in President Biden a while ago. It is time for Joe Biden to give it up. As of today, all of the polls are favoring My Quarterback, Donald J. Trump. Just walk away Joe, it's all over. This screen call was unsuccessful and did not end with a touchdown, it ended with a Democratic meltdown. Go Trump 2024!

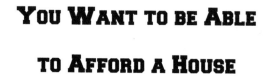

You Want to be Able to Afford a House

Vote Trump

2024

CHAPTER 21

THE PLAY: HALF BRO (OBAMA) TO HALF BRO (TRUMP) HANDOFF:

What's happening Bro, we need to talk. We made history together Bro. I remember seeing you at Calypso Café in Chicago back in the day. That was some delicious ass food! I'm a proud truck driver. I also would like to commend you on your rendition of Al Green *Let's Stay Together.* I'm more of a Marvin Gaye fan, *What's Going On*, you feel me. They are both awesome. Let's stay together is kinda what I'm writing about Bro.

To hell with Let's stay Together, not Al Green, but you lousy do-nothing Democrats. I'm leaving the party Bro! Its Maga Time Bro! As I alluded to, I'm a truck driver. That highway that is named after you in Illinois has a very bumpy right lane Bro. Can you tell the road crew to handle that for me. One more thing about your singing, you sound like Usher Bro!

Your Democratic party policies are killing the owner-operator truck driver. Remember, we are an essential service, with and without covid. As an owner-operator truck driver, it is our responsibility to pay for all expenses incurred to operate our vehicles which include tractor trailers, straight trucks, cargo vans and more. I'm writing to you because President Biden does not even know which way is up or down for real, for real.

The entire Democratic Party needs to be impeached/prosecuted and criminally charged for fraud and deceit. The American people have been hoodwinked by the Democratic Party. Our country has a Manchurian President. It's being governed by a committee of Democratic Progressive lunatics clowns that are destroying the country. Let me be clear, we were better off with Trump policies, I'm talking about the whole world.

Back in the year 2017 when the ceremonial transfer of power occurred at the Whitehouse, I felt a sense of pride. I voted for change with President Obama for two terms, Did change occur? That is highly debatable. I voted for President Trump because I felt supremely confident that monumental change would occur with President Trump. President Trump seemed like the type of man that would implement his agenda no matter the opposition he would be confronted with.

President Trump had to deal with a gauntlet of the highest order of Democratic bullshit, along with some rhino Republicans. Like Big Daddy Kane, the rapper, he got the job done. As a result, our country prospered. This is a fact. The world was not on fire like it is today under Joe Biden's administration. Trump is My Quarterback aka President 2024!

Chapter 22

Trucker BG on the Citizens Band Radio:

Everyday Trucker: "Breaker, braker one-nine, you out there Trucker BG, c'mon?"

Trucker BG: "Trucker BG here, what's your handle (name) c'mon?"

Everyday Trucker: "Everyday Trucker here, just a rolling on down to Fresno in my new rig, I got me one of those flat beds."

"Where you headed and what you rolling in trucker BG, c'mon?"

Trucker BG: " I'm rolling on out to Scranton, PA in my Stewart Baker pick-up truck, you copy? "

Everyday Trucker: "Goddamn Trucker BG, the only thang you can haul is influence and that small bag of cocaine they found at the Whitehouse.

Breaker, Breaker one-nine, Hey Trucker BG, does that BG in your handle stand for Bug Guy, as in Joe Biden, copy?"

Trucker BG: "That's a big 10-4!"

Everyday Trucker: "Well I'll be! Put them ears on trucker bros, we got that fake ass President and half ass truck driver out here. Run his ass back to Delaware. That Mofo ain't worth one anorexic hog. This is Trump Country!"

CHAPTER 23

THE VERDICT

Its May 30, 2024 @11:57 pm. As I sit here in the coin operated retro laundromat three minutes before midnight, I am waiting for the washing machine to release the dirt and grime from my work clothes. I feel myself getting frustrated by the news on the television monitors on the wall. Special Report stating the Guilty verdict. All ten monitors are on the same bullshit. No cable in this old retro laundromat, just the old legacy media democratic apparatchiks.

Just like the old coin operated washing machines are spinning dirt, so is the legacy media. Never mind that there have been various instances in this case where Trump's rights were violated. Never mind the finance election official expert was not allowed to be an expert witness. Motherfuck trying to disenfranchise one half of the population of the country. Also, the total disregard for the statute of limitations. All while totally looking the other way regarding the Big Guys bogus wealth accumulation scheme. Way to go cover uppers. Hey Mr. Network CEO, you wonder why you are losing viewership. Listen to this truck driver. Stop bullshiting and be objective. You all sound like a bunch of well groomed, extensive vocabulary parrots, polly wants a cracker, you hear the reverb.

If it was not for my QB your networks would have a zero Nielson rating.

PUT AMERICA FIRST!

TRUMP 2024

Chapter 24

Multi- Cultural Citizens Lament:

English: Leave the democratic party now! Vote For Trump 2024

Spanish: deja el partido democrático ahora, Vote For Trump 2024

Italian: lasciate subito il partito democratico, Vote For Trump 2024

French: quitte le parti démocrate maintenant, Vote For Trump 2024

Polish: opuścić teraz partię demokratyczną, Vote For Trump 2024

Leave the Lousy Do Nothing Democratic Party: The Party that destroys everything it touches. Which includes: cities, schools, the law, sports, politics, churches and more.

APPENDIX

You Call the Play Game

The game where you call the play for My Quarterback, Donald John Trump to get the U.S. Best Policy Zone for the touchdown. The following are the instructions:

1. The line of scrimmage always starts at mid-field or the fifty-yard line.

2. Put on your offensive coordinator hat and choose 4 plays from the listing of plays to select. Each play has a corresponding yardage number. For Example, if you select screen play and the corresponding yardage is 4, you gained 4 yards. If the number was zero, you did not gain any yardage and its now second down.

   Just like real football, if you can gain 10 yards on a play, you get 4 new sets of plays that you can select.

   Just like real football, if you do not get 10 yards using any of your initial 4 sets of plays, you lose the game.

3. You can play as many time's you want using the plays that you have not selected.

4. When your yardage is more than 50 yards, you have scored a touchdown.

PLAY LISTING

- Play Action
- Double Reverse
- Hook and Ladder
- Screen
- Trap Run
- Slant Route
- Whip Route
- Shovel Pass
- Go Route
- End-Around
- Run-Pass Option
- Double Slant Route
- Dig Route
- Halfback Option Play
- Out Route
- Flea-Flicker
- Statute of Liberty
- Stick Route
- Curl Route
- Fly Pattern

GAME ONE PLAY YARDAGE LISTING

PLAY	YARDAGE
Play Action	7 yards
Hook and Ladder	15 yards
Screen	0 yards
Trap Run	1 yard
Slant Route	0 yards
Whip Route	15 yards
Shovel Pass	3 yards
Go Route	35 yards
End -Around	0 yards
Run-Pass Option	1 yard
Double Slant Route	7 yards
Dig Route	35 yards
Halfback Option Play	0 yards
Out Route	0 yards
Flea- Flicker	0 yards
Stick Route	35 yards
Curl Route	7 yards
Fly Pattern	0 yards
Statue of Liberty	15 yards
Double Reverse	3 yards

ACCESS GAME TWO ON THE FOLLOWING PAGE

GAME TWO PLAY YARDAGE LISTING

PLAY	YARDAGE
Play Action	10 yards
Hook and Ladder	17 yards
Screen	5 yards
Trap Run	2 yards
Slant Route	7 yards
Whip Route	8 yards
Shovel Pass	2 yards
Go Route	12 yards
End -Around	16 yards
Run-Pass Option	5 yards
Double Slant Route	10 yards
Dig Route	20 yards
Halfback Option Play	0 yards
Out Route	0 yards
Flea- Flicker	0 yards
Stick Route	8 yards
Curl Route	19 yards
Fly Pattern	25 yards
Statue of Liberty	0 yards
Double Reverse	15 yards

SOURCE PAGE

U.S. House Committee on Ways Democrats Cannot change the Biden-Harris Record of High Prices
July 26,2024
U.S. Agency of International Development

MR-Mag.com
August 14,2020

Abc7Chicago Digital Team
August 16, 2023

Fox 32 Chicago
By Kasey Chronis
April 4, 2022

The 10 worst things President Biden Did in 2023
The Washington Post
By Marc A. Thiessen

Jim Clyburn changed everything for Joe Bidens's campaign . He's been a political force for a long time
The Washington Post by Donna M. Owens
April 1, 2020

AUTHOR'S BIO

Looking through the prism of a truck windshield, the author draws upon his everyday encounters, routines, and observations as a truck driver in Illinois. He combines his three favorite passions, American Football,satire and Presidential Politics. Until the next chapter, this is not Bill Kurtis, its Brian E. Davis

Contact
Email Address: AuthorBrianEDavis@yahoo.com

Milton Keynes UK
Ingram Content Group UK Ltd.
UKHW020056181024
449757UK00011B/647